Of Jíbaros and Hillbillies

Ricardo Nazario y Colón

Plain View Press
P. O. 42255
Austin, TX 78704

plainviewpress.net
sb@plainviewpress.net
512-441-2452

ISBN: 978-1-935514-13-8
Library of Congress Number: 2010939023

Cover design by Holly Thompson, Htphoto.design@gmail.com

Acknowledgements

I am grateful to the editors of these publications for giving my work a home.

"We Raised You," *Aphros Review, Fall 1995*; "Defiance," *Art Scene, Fall 2009*; "Silence in the Mountain," *Art Scene, Fall 2009*; "Tennessee Trace," *Art Scene, Fall 2009*; "Open Mind Tanganyika," *Art Scene, Fall 2009*; "Appalachian Atronachs," *Art Scene, Fall 2009*; "Tujcalusa," *Louisville Review, Fall 2009*; "Up North," *Falling Star Magazine, Spring/Summer 2005*; "Prelude to a Revolution," *Nappy New Millennium, Spring 1998*; "The Panther within US," *Nappy New Millennium, Spring 1998*; "When I get Back," *A Hudson View, Summer 2010*.

Contents

With Gratitude

Este poemario esta completamente dedicado a mi madre Francisca Colón López a quien le debo la deuda mas grande del mundo, mi vida.

My gratitude to everyone listed below for your contribution to the man that I am today.

My grandparents, aunts, uncles, cousins and the rest of my family Roberto, Oscar, Jonath (Ismael), Maritza, Solmelissa, Wanda, Corey and Ivette. To my daughter Rian Penman and my son Carlos Francisco Nazario-Goodwin. To Faye Smith and my Danville, KY family. To Shon and the Goodwin family, to the Velazquez family, to Orlando and family, to Michael and the Johnson Family, to T.S.D.

With love, and loyalty for my poetic family who birthed me, nurtured me and gave me permission to write; the Affrilachian Poets: Frank X Walker, Nikky Finney, Mitchell L.H. Douglas, Daundra Harden, Kelly Ellis, Gerald Coleman, Thomas Aaron, Crystal Wilkinson, Paul Taylor, Bernard Clay, Jude McPherson, Lerim Kol, Dan Wu, Paul Taylor, Shanna Smith, Miysan Crosswhite, Jahi Chikwendu, Bianca Spriggs, Asha French, Parneshia Jones, Hao Wang, Stewart Stone, Tania James, Amanda Johnston, Christine Rose James, Tony Rawlings, Sam Fitzpatrick, Shayla Lawson, Ellen Hagan, Stephanie Pruitt, Crystal Good, Natasha Marin, Marta Miranda, Makalani Bandele, Keith Wilson, Norman Jordan, Hasan Davis, Joy K. Gonsalves and Rane Arroyo.

Super special thanks to Bianca Spriggs, Tracy N. Bonilla and Lisa Alvarado for your editorial help.

Thank you for inspiring me Mr. Medina and the Lou Gehrig I.S. 151. To my first grade teacher Mrs. Rosa for your lessons on humanity and the Jesús T. Piñero school. For the shapers of DeWitt Clinton Men: Jim Garvey and Bert Blanco for seeing our potential beyond sports. For el Barrío Carruzos, Carolina de Puerto Rico and 115 McClellan St in The Bronx, NYC places where poetry is found in the moisture of the air. To Fordham University, Hudson Valley Community College, University of Kentucky, Pace University and Western Kentucky University for lessons in the classroom and in life. To Keely and John Steele owners of Tricky Fish and The Bluegrass

Kitchen and to the community of Charleston, West Virginia because I feel so much at home when I'm with you. The U.S. Marine Corps for the lessons and value of repetitious training. The Mu Iota, Mu Theta, and Epsilon Sigma, Eta Alpha Sigma chapters of Phi Beta Sigma Fraternity, Inc. for raising my racial consciousness and for Zeta Phi Beta Sorority, Inc. To Kentucky, for allowing me to be part of the building of a New Kentucky Home. To Agatha and María, with this book I am keeping my promise.

To my special supporters Denise Johnson-Kleberg, Tanya R. Johnson, Ed Velazquez, Don McDaniels, Jessica Bell, and Marta Miranda.

A Note On Caribbean Spanish, With Special Consideration Given To That Of Puerto Rico

The nature of language is, on the one hand, highly fluid. As anyone who has read Shakespeare or Twain knows, the meaning, the spelling, even the pronunciation of words change over time. Furthermore, languages constantly borrow words from other languages to supplement a lack of expression or precision: canoe and barbeque not only came into English from Spanish but they came into Spanish from Taíno and Arawak, the native languages of the people who lived in the Caribbean basin before the Spanish conquest. The fluidity of language does not only have to do with changes over time, but also an individual speaker can learn to alter patterns of speech and/or "code-switch"—that is move from standard usage to either another language or non-standard usage, move from one dialect of a language to another—in order to better fit in with specific social groups or emphasize certain social or political points. Despite this mutability, certain traits seem almost constant and give a specific local flavor to regional dialects.

The Spanish of the conquistadors was hardly uniform. During the years when Spain took possession of the Western Hemisphere and conquered its peoples, the Iberian Peninsula was home to many different dialects and several independent languages, whether of Latin origin or not. The provenance of the various conquistadors, coupled with the native languages, and, depending on the region of Latin America, the importation of Africans as slave-labor all left their mark on the language spoken by the inhabitants of those regions.

The two major dialects of Spanish that principally have influenced the Caribbean dialect are the Andalusian and Canary Islander. Not only did the vast majority of early Spanish settlers of the Caribbean basin come from these two regions—which were both seafaring and of warmer climate than other parts of Spain—, immigration from both Andalusia and the Canary Islands continued throughout the 19th century well into the early 20th. Cuba and Puerto Rico, it should be remembered, remained highly profitable colonies of Spain until the Spanish American War in 1898. Indeed, the trace of these dialects can still be heard: the nasalization of words ending in /n/ (San Juan becomes something like *Sang Juang*), the aspiration, or swallowing, of the final /s/ (*nosotros* becomes *nosotro*), the elision of final the /r/ (*volver* becomes *volvé*), or even the switching of the /r/ for the /l/ and vice versa (*puerta* becomes *puelta* or *volver* becomes *vorver*).

To focus solely on the influence of variants of Iberian Spanish, however, is to ignore the significant linguistic contributions of those of African descent and even the possibility of traces of Taíno or Arawak on the Spanish of the Greater Antilles. In regards to native languages, it is difficult to ascribe anything beyond loan words—canoe, barbeque, hammock, etc. The case of African languages, however, is different.

Indeed, the discovery and colonization of the New World and the massive enslavement of Africans for labor purposes is almost one and the same story. The rapid depletion of the native population, due to European illnesses and forced labor, quickly lead to the importation of Africans. The first Africans arrived in the Caribbean at the dawn of the 16th century, less than a decade after the first Spanish ships stumbled upon the West Indies. They were brought to work the gold-fields promised by Columbus in his first letters of discovery and by the end of the century were being employed on plantations of various sorts—sugar, indigo, etc. The last slave ship arrived in Cuba in 1866, a good forty years after Spain had signed a treaty with England to abolish the slave trade three and a half centuries after the first ship brought enslaved Africans to the Caribbean.

Assessing the specific influence that African languages have had on the Spanish of the Caribbean basin, beyond certain lexical borrowings and colloquialisms—*bemba*, for lips, or *chévere*, for cool or awesome, or *bochinche*, for gossip—, has proven quite difficult and contentious. Certain phonetic traits, nasalization of the final /n/, the aspiration of the /s/, the elision of the intervocalic /d/ (*estado* becomes *estao*), the switching of the /r/ for the /l/, though not necessarily vice versa, have all been ascribed to African influence. Many of these traits, as already discussed, can be found in the Andalusian and Canary Islander dialects. Thus, certain scholars have been quite reticent to attribute any sort of phonetic influence on Caribbean Spanish from African languages. It should be remembered, though, that these two regions of Spain, especially the Canary Islands, have historically had considerable contact with African peoples. Also, the processes of dialect formation are messy; it is quite possible to have more than one origin for the same phenomenon.

Despite similarities, especially between and among the Greater Antilles, each nation, island, region of the Caribbean has its own dialect that contains traces of that region's history. Though to someone not from the region, Cuban, Dominican, and Puerto Rican Spanish might seem indistinguishable, there are variances, rhythms, intonations that readily identify island of origin.

Ricardo Nazario y Colón is of Puerto Rican descent and grew up in the Puerto Rican enclave of the South Bronx. His spoken Spanish retains the speech rhythms and patterns of intonation of Puerto Rico. Also, having grown up in a bilingual setting, code-switching, from English to Spanish and back again in the same conversation and/or sentence, is simply the way language is used among his own. Though code-switching is motivated by a host of conscious and unconscious reasons, it cannot be denied that language and ethnic groups code-switch and pepper their speech with words from the culturally non-dominant language to make social and political points. Language, thus, becomes a means of resisting the imposition of a dominant narrative and of asserting, validating, and celebrating an identity that is not always sanctioned by the culture at large.

Though it is impossible to reproduce the rhythms of his speech on the printed page, certain traits, such as the elision of a consonant or entire syllables, the aspiration of a vowel, even the shift of an /r/ to an /l/, can be represented graphically. In his collection "Of Jíbaros and Hillbillies," Nazario y Colón bears witness to the particularities of the Puerto Rican dialect. For example, in the poem "Escarmiento" he shortens words by eliminating whole syllables. Some good examples are the words *nada* (nothing) and *para* (for) become *na* and *pa*. In "I Still Wonder" he also employs debuccalization, that is where a consonant like /s/, /f/, or /th/ become an /h/ or a glottal stop. For example, *estar*, to be, is *ejtal*, where the /s/ becomes /j/ and should be pronounced as an h. Also, as characteristic of Puerto Rican Spanish, the /r/ mutates to /l/.

Not only does his collection attempt to capture the speech patterns of Puerto Ricans and Nuyoricans, his use of code-switching provides eloquent testimony to the way bilingual groups employ language. Throughout "Of Jíbaros and Hillbillies," intimate moments, whether involving religious practices, like Catholic prayers or Santería rituals, or the passing down of wisdom from the older generation to the younger, the extolling of another's beauty, the private language of lovers, or the bearing witness to domestic joys and pains, are recorded in Spanish rather than English. The effect is that of passing on an open secret—open because the poet is using language to confess the impressions left and emotions felt during these moments, secret because the reader must know the code/language to access the information.

Nazario y Colón's poetry, through code-switching, through use of non-standard Spanish, and even non-standard English, interrogates the relationship between language and poetry. Must the code-switching poet travel only between polished and purified languages, using only the king's English, only the queen's Spanish? Poetry is the artful use of language to bear witness to the human experience. Thus, it should be expansive enough to include within it the use of multiple languages, popular speech, the speech of non-dominant groups, even so-called solecisms. Must the poet tame and purify the language of his community in order to achieve art? In this case, Nazario y Colón's poems show us that poetry is generous enough embrace the use of "imperfect" language, so that art, so that poetry, rather than hiding imperfection, highlights the beauty of imperfection in order to better bear witness to the language, the culture, the experience of a community.

Jeremy Paden, Ph.D.
Assistant Professor of Spanish
and Latin American Literature and Culture,
Transylvania University

Bendición

Escarmiento

I keep a glass rock, bamboo and a cowry shell
in my Juju. Yesterday, I found it on my bed
slightly opened, smelling of Tamarindo and Guanabana.
My grandmother's wisdom reminded me
why it hung on my wall;
how it helped to keep the Devil out of my house.

Agüela was a Christian but the Yoruba in her,
harked back through prayer and holy things.
Across coffee and sugar cane fields,
to a place where her grandchildren saw
the evil that saunter among them.

When Agüela talked, *yo me quedaba eleto,*
out of respect and out of fear because demons
and such things *se aparecían como si na.*
Tocando puerta, pretending not to bother,
necesitando something unimportant like,
un cafesito o una azuquita. En escarmiento, she told me,
nunca lo recibas en la puelta de atrás.

She did not need to explain,
but she made it clear, never to receive
whoever might be the devil at the back door.
She crossed herself as if in prayer.
Uttering in her raspy tobacco voice,
"Ay Jesú Manifica!"
She always crossed herself when
she talked about the devil.

I opened my juju and everything I kept inside was there;
the glass rock, the bamboo, the cowry shell.

Agüela spoke with a teacher's clarity,
beware, *"el Diablo es hombre y mujel."*
Everything it touches smells of *Tamarindo y Guanábana,*
"pero ese dulce es pa' esconder la pejte en su corazón."
To protect the family's honor she said, *"entiera la taza*
en el batey, donde Facundo ya no mete la aza."

"Mira, nunca-never take your eyes off the devil."
She cast her long gaze through the window
and follows him, while praying in Spanish
and sometimes in Yoruba, for Facundo
her husband, father of nine, Agüelo,
who worked as a *Taladol,* not to see him
leaving the house.

Today, there are times when I cross myself
because you never know how or when
the devil will try to enter your house.

I remember Agüela sitting on her rocking chair
gazing one hundred years out of the window,
recordandose de lo Yoruba.
Agüela speaks to me, *"Algo se quema mijito."*

I put the Juju back on the wall
and make my way towards the door.
Ahí esta la Tipa de next-door; ejtá por la maceta.
Agüela's words guide my hand; I leave the chain
on the door; she sees my left eye.
"¿Con permiso, tiene uste café?" I think fast,
"No, yo no tomo café."

I close my door con *la cerradura, el cuartón, la aldaba,*
el police lock, *la cadena y dejo mis purmones caer.*
Through the peephole I watch her disappear.
I lean my forehead against the door and think
of my grandmother rocking by her open window;
I cross myself. *"Ay Jesú Manifica!"*

Agüela dice, *"en paredes cubiertas demonios no entran."*
I always keep the juju on the wall.

Invierno

The epiphany celebration;
when three kings traversed the great desert,
a reminder it was winter
and we were not going to the beach.

Instead we prayed over;
seven rosaries; one holy bead at a time
a la santa maria madre de dio
ruega pol nosotro pecadore
ahora in la hora de nuejtra muelte.

Her chilled skin soft like the mud
where yucca grows, was not due to the season
but to *la muelte.*

Years on this earth were marked
by shades of gold in her wrinkles;
by a tobacco stained smile that removed
the etching of my finger prints from the pews.

It was winter finally,
for she who poured warm smiles
and generosity into our coffee cups.

The honey locust and patchouli trees
will continue to shade her side of the street
and I will forever be *su nieto.*

We Raised You

My griot told me
we did not raise you that way—

    hating those you've never known,
    taking the breath of life on lovers' day,
    turning your back on your own—

She told me about our ways.

She went back six generations explaining
how her grandfather's skin was like caoba and his hair—

    curling her index finger to leave a tiny hole—
was like little caracolitos.

My griot told me
José was a distinguido African man
who worked from sun-up to sun-down,
walking many miles to and from work,
never forgetting to feed the animals;
chickens, cows and pigs.
Took time to love the woman
who made sure he would squeeze
three hours of rest somewhere
in between the stacks of sugar cane.
The same woman who gifted him
six reminders of the motherland.

My griot told me
we celebrate *el día de la raza.*
Explained how agüelos mother was Taína—

    con *la piel de canela*
    and that beautiful long hair—
    covering her back like a queens royal gown—

I used to wash it, comb it
and twist it into the crown
she wore while watching
the creator's wonders rise and set.

She taught me about my three times great grandfather,
a handsome preacher man—
    un Ejpañol alto—
as tall as the horse he rode on his wedding day,
who used his divine prayers, to catch snakes.

I learned the story of *el tuco* snake!
Which came calling for my *tatara visa agüelo*, a preacher.
Not a southern grits, eggs and ham preacher,
who has the congregation swaying like Jonah
in that ship, but an island *vianda and verdura* preacher,
that fills the aisle with the holy ghost
and spends the afternoon fanning the congregation.

The story began with a young snake, caught
in between machete strikes on a burning afternoon
at the cane fields. It ended with the tuco on the yard
and the twenty country feet long father gone—
after a three hour prayer of salvation.

My griot told me
we did not raise you that way!
Love-less, faith-less, culture-less
she said, love up, pray up, wake
up 'cause,
we'll always raise you straight
and now it's your turn,
to keep the winds whispering our ways.

How Deep Is Your Love

Asking for mercy from the creator, for speaking ill of the dead

I leaned on the bureau
playing with the bottles of perfume.
Invisible yo era escuchando a mi mai llorrar.

It was not a surprising betrayal
for a marriage of convenience.

From New York he said,
we would be taken care of.
Okay if she found herself another man
brought the most tears to her eyes.

We were the bastard children—
Our father was— a photograph,
a last name, an emerald on a ring.

"As long as no one knows," he said.

How could a man want to be a *Cabrón!*
His woman, his wife, my mother
una puta, ella no era.

When sins mattered and single mothers
could be socially stoned.
At that time— she put her life on a shelf,
divorced his sorry ass and devoted
all that she was— to raise us.
Not knowing it would last forever.

Monthly photo shoots, three-piece suits,
fresh hair cuts, and lots of Alberto vo.5
were her promise, to not let her pain
be more than a menstrual reminder.

Our tiny hands scribbled love letters
to photographs that did not hug us back.

In the night we lay awake whispering
how sad were the songs in her bedroom.
In the morning Mami's smile
would make everything feel good
and for another day— childhood was happiness.

Unassigned

So many things went unassigned
like the ironing of clothes,
and the washing of dishes.
Hope was a twisted strip of paper in a
green Export Soda cracker can.
There were no conversations about
how to apply all temperature Cheer;
ayudenme a doblar la ropa was a suggestion.

Though she did not read product labels
her olfaction was a Geiger counter at
impoverished supermarkets who purveyed
unwanted cuts of meat soaked in bleached
to mask their decaying state.

On Three Kings day, there were gifts
not of myrrh, incense or gold but
calzoncillos, camisetas, y camisas
for children not born in mangers.

A sunflower pot adorned the fire escape window,
where there was no vegetable garden,
tilling of the soil, or waiting
for the sun to dry the earth.

No one suffered from Anosmia *cuando
se escuchaban gritos de fuego en el 23,
cuando el estiércol de flores volaba
entre las brisas de humo negro.*

*Hoy, aunque no se pronuncial las palabras
que nunca escuché, se que hay niños
con mucho menos* than I ever had
and I look back with a grateful heart
contemplating, how much less she grew up with.

Witness

She faced him down in the middle of the road
drunken with love, with fear of loneliness,
confused by a sense of fighting for what
she thought belong to her, not expecting
a pistol's bullet to open her flesh.

I saw the bitter rage of his blind eye.
As he drove off, with no concern we fixed gazes.
Locked and loaded on my ten year old gawkiness,
his twenty something eyes engraved my record.

I felt hollow in places I did not recognized;
franticly searching where her body had fallen.
I was lassoed away with my brothers to safety.
No words could explain the bullet and her disappearance.

Clouds hovered like birds of prey during the day.
At night behind wrought iron our perimeter
was delineated by watchful eyes and a rusted pistol,
who ordered us when to go inside.

I imagined her soul like a runaway slave
traveling at night, through cow pastures
and behind barbwire; deep in the snake filled woods;
sleeping on impromptu beds of leaves.

Giving her pound of flesh, trying to reach
her Underground Railroad haven. Almost
suffocating under a laundry breastplate
inside of a cardboard box.

Hearing our voices, "Have you seen mami?"
Wanting to reach out to us;
knowing she had to wait for the storm to pass
before she could dance with us.

Chiro

A short chiseled man with copper plated skin
and the gift of embellishment.
Favorite uncle, he lived a solemn life.

In another time he was married to Cali,
the most beautiful and classical lady
ever to have been attached to our family.

On fate day she learned a four-floor window
at 110th St. and Manhattan Ave. in Harlem
was her freedom.

The grown-ups talked in whispers about it;
Chiro never did.

I Still Wonder

After Carmen Nereida Figueroa

The narrow path still turns into a creek
when the rainy season comes.
The last time I stood at the bottom of the path
the house was not there anymore.

It was a one room wooden house painted yellow
that stood on stilts near the top of the hill.
Its most beautiful attribute was a three quarter
veranda where I imagined God resting
on a hammock commanding the cool winds
to swoop upon it and it was a wonderful place.

We spent many days there with my uncle
including January 13th 1978.
I remember the sun, the hummingbirds
by the flame tree and how we gathered
as if playing marbles in a circle.
In it stood my uncle Chiro, my cousins
Angelo and Pin and Anibal, a childhood friend.

We were having a carefree conversation
with my uncle and talked about how termites
were eating away at the wooden stilts
that propped up the house and we laughed
at the prospects of it being consumed in one day.

In a moment everything stopped
as Anibal's brother Junior in a rush, out of breath
and paled face, made his way to us.

"Chiro!
La casa de Mael se cayo y mato a Nereida!"

My uncle Mael's house had collapsed
and my aunt had been killed.

The hummingbirds slowed before my eyes.
Chiro ushered himself to his feet.

"Ay Dio! Hay que il pa-ya!"

Those were the last words I heard
for the time it took me to run the 300 feet
down the narrow path to my home.
At the bottom an eight-foot chain link fence awaited
but it did not matter to my arms and legs
for they were vaulting me before I could command them.

Junior's words echoed out in my mother's kitchen
as she was preparing that evenings meal.

"Mami! La casa de Mael se cayo y mato a Nereida!"

Things fell.

"Qué? Quién Dijo?"
"Junior, todo el mundo va pa-ya."

José Luis my mother's boyfriend
grabbed the keys to the 1975 Royal Blue Beattle.

"Yo se lo dije que dejara de ejtal catando debajo desa casa."

His was another voice, another warning
unheard by the stubbornness of man.
We rode up the hill street in the Volky
with it's distinct engine sound,
making eye contact with my cousins and friends
as they ran along the bamboo lined street.

The numbness of the reality was approaching,
for this had been any other instance
we would have given anyone a ride.

The neighborhood's rollercoaster turn
was a place we new would reveal
the unbelievable truth meanwhile,
we kept noticing the migration of friends
and neighbors from behind barbwire fields
and across the Pangola.

The echoes waiting to be released
fell out of our throats at the turn on the road.
The simultaneous sound of *ay dioj mio, tu vej*
allowed us the passage traffic would not.
We ran the last few hundred yards.
Wounded by the scene I became
a shadow among hundreds. Moving about,

watching my grandfather trying to raise the house
with his crowbar; listening to my uncle's tears
scream in my grandmother's arms.
Asking myself why everyone was watching?
Could they not see her feet move below
the mass of cinder blocks and concrete?

Onlookers created a natural perimeter;
the cross of the Eben-Ezer Evangelical church
towered over the scene from across the street
and I wondered as my aunt lie beneath;
as on lookers whispered the futility
of my grandfather's crowbar;
if the strength of Samson, of all the men gathered,
could lift the crumbled house?
But we all stayed on the perimeter, watching
my grandfather and his crowbar.

El Don

For Solmelissa Colón y Figueroa

I once dreamt of Piñones and shared it with her.
A place I have never been. I stood gazing
at its dirty waters and all the people in it.

She told me that dirty water meant death was coming.
We both said *"Ojalá que no sea yo."* Calling on Allah's
protection like Puerto Ricans always do.

My son Carlos, reminds me of you,
of how you used to follow her steps.
And I think of the day— of your age—

of how she sat you next to Maritza and Tito
on the old car seat by the side of the house.
She was going inside to prepare coffee.

Agüela speaks to me from many years ago,
with words that keep her alive in me. Sometimes,
I hear the grown ups whisper of your Don

and I smile—because I know of you—
of what you conjured up to keep her bound to us.
Of special places where only you— get to feel her touch.

Today, when the ground shakes
I close my eyes and I listen for your whispers.
and she returns to me; a sunflower in the sun.

Defiance

Morning once again; children roaming the house,
"Has anyone seen my shoes?"
chorus response, *NO!*

America is under siege
by TV coverage of D.C. sniper.

The sound of metal rubbing on metal
brings everything to a holt.
A special report: F.B.I. releasing latest composite.

America waits in anticipation and I
cross my fingers like I always do

whispering a prayer yet again to GOD,
"Please don't let him be—"

Hazelnut filters through the air
and a flash sketch appears of a middle aged
white man—
deep breath is released.

Metal on metal begins rubbing into motion;
America gets back to its daily grind.

Suddenly, hurricane large, my daughter screams,
"Why! Why can't it be a woman?"

I stop, I look, I sketch her;
profiling a pre teen, and her world.
Realizing she is live flesh standing arms stiff
at her side, fist clench and muscles pulsating
underneath her tiny Catholic school uniform.

Understanding that part of who she is as woman
coming into being is the assumed invisibility
of her existence by numbers and probabilities.

Hide and Go Seek

For Charlie "Papón" Colón my namesake "Kayuka" 1961-2008

As children we played at night
behind barb wire fenced woods.

The crick of our bodies sometimes gave
dried leaves a reason to reveal our presence.

You was the most committed. Plunging deeper
past the spider webs and hollow snake logs.

We played like there was a grand prize;
some life altering reward for Jíbaros kids.

Although we expected everyone to return,
we usually rescued you from deep in the woods.

Southern Exposure

Silence In the Mountain

It is not the shock or disbelief that has numbed
every hill and dale on my body. Nor can I say
that these men and women whom I have sheltered
for generations hate me.

I want to forget, but on my best day the sound
of metal, a vibration on the road, or the smell of asphalt
brings it all back, and I feel like its happening
again and again.

Sometimes, no matter how many times I wash my face
the smell of gasoline remains and my wrists burn.
These sensations are overwhelming and they cling to me
like a deep despair that disconnects me from this reality
and I pray for everything to just, pour out.

With each minute I learn to survive
even though part of myself has been stripped, lost.
My body wakes me at the same time that it happened.
It's not the headaches or the bellyaches
that make things difficult—it's the loss.

Every night when the moon chases the sun from my sky,
I search for my mountain; I look in the brooks and under the brush.
There is shame in my movements now,
strangers see the change in me and choose not to visit
and I wonder if they think I am damaged goods.

In some way I feel responsible. I must have seduced them.
Perhaps my pristine beauty was too alluring
and I took it and them for granted.

I just wish— I could stop feeling dirty.
That my sense of worth was higher.
That every stare was not one of pity or judgment.

It's been nearly ninety years
and it seems like it will never go away.
But I've learned not to think about it —everyday— anymore.

Tennessee Trace

It is the rumor, the hollow stare,
the specter of dust that guides me to the mouth
of the Buffalo river.

There, the water trembles with echoes
of Generals Hood and Beull
and if your eyes are closed enough—
you can catch a face full of wind
sweeping from over the bent backs of trees,
who still shiver at the scent
of the old iron Napier Furnace
burning their kin.

The road tells me of native voices living
near the salt lick where the buffalo traced;
it is not written on asphalt or signs,
yet I know of fallen leaves,
the snap of trees and the broken faces—
on the side of this road.

Appalachian Atronachs

They wear their armor like full body tattoos,
blasting illiteracy with lyrics and stanzas.

On No/Yes avenue in Charleston, inside a middle school
their magicka conjures possibility.
In alter ego garb they move around town unnoticed,
fueling their super human strength from the potential
of young Affrilachian children in after school bunkers.

When these unmasked avengers combine
their elemental skills and healing abilities, minds
are transformed into libraries of ancient scrolls.

Teaming with local Mages who are emblazoned with Keloids,
reminders of the battles being fought to protect
the next generation, from becoming coal gathering hatchlings.
These Atronachs engage the roar of the coal dragons,
striking underneath their scales with the accuracy of Marksmen.

They are masterminds, shape shifters, and slashers.
Speeding in and out of West Virginia mining towns and Kentucky
hollers fighting despair and infusing hearts with hope and trust.

Not Gadgeteers or Mechanized Machine Pilots,
who invoke no power of their own, but Mentalists,
heroes with the ability to move hearts with their words.

I call them poets, ordinary human beings
with the most powerful ability in the known universe, love.

Black Belly

At times she wobbles in discomfort,
when chiseled men meander into her belly.

It reminds her of stories from back
in the salt lake days out west.

She has never been accused of being undisciplined,
disagreeable, or uncompassionate.

Hers is a tale of adventure, and openness,
one that invigorates the spirit with inspiration.

It's the beckoning that brings them into her womb.
These interlopers and addicts can't refuse what grows within.

Drunken with emotion, blinded by coal's rewards,
they slither their way far beyond where she is comfortable.

These ground hogs believe they know her
and bathe in a false sense of experience.

Sometimes they treat her with suspicion and antagonism,
just because she doesn't always want to be stimulated.

It is during these moments that she may act neurotic
and swears they are calling her emotionally unstable.

So she swallows a handful of them,
as a reminder of the kind of woman she once was.

In the Beginning

No matter how deeply you pick to the bone,
she is the color of copper.
Her distinguishing features are rugged,
tall and craggy.

Hers is a story written in sediment layers,
in circles beneath the bark of trees
and by the smoothing power of water.

She was there when the almighty sat down
to rest at Lebanon Valley, flattening her,
watched Mounts Washington and Mitchell
wear down to stumps prior to the passing
of the dinosaurs.

Opened up her streams for the brook trout
to escape the great freeze,
said hello to the Himalayas before
they were a whisper and bequeathed
Chomolungma the sky.

She watched animals become men
with erect backs and spines
and then built a great wall
to keep one another apart.

Before Persia swept across the Middle East
expanse and the Romans created a continent,
she stood watch over the Taíno, Olmec and Maya.

Before the Cherokee scratched her face,
her veins pulsed with coal.

What Can Brown Do For You?

Brown doesn't know when or why **Brown** was born?
Sometimes, **Brown** lives and feels like a stranger.

Brown doesn't always have a bed to wake up in.
A **brown** cardboard box is where **Brown** lives.
Much of the food **Brown** eats is **brown.**
People move away when they see **Brown** coming.

Daring, fearless, adventurous; walking, running,
riding across the deserts because **Brown**
is committed to family survival.

There are times when **Brown** dies packed like cattle
in train cars and no one knows or cares
until it smells like dead **Brown.**

Brown works hard building houses, washing plates,
picking tobacco, keeping grounds, grooming horses,
making crazy love to your daughter or son,
sometimes even your wife.

In the morning, before reminding the rooster it's time to crow
and after a sixteen hour work day,
Brown rejoices with a cold beer and a full plate of **brown** rice.

Even when you wash and polish **Brown,**
Brown can still be sweaty, smelly and dirty.
It is almost like **Brown** is **brown.**

Brown's car is nice with hydraulics that make **Brown**
seem taller and wireless sounds for **Brown** to listen to—
    The Moody **Brown**s
    Lady Sings the **Brown**s
    and Little Boy **Brown**

These **brown** sounds were a gift from **Brown** chocolate—
wrapped in a pretty **brown** paper bag
with a matching **brown** lasso and a happy
three kings day let's make **brown** babies note.

Though the season wasn't **brown** enough
and they really weren't kings but three fit the theme,
the celebration is stilled honored because to **Brown**
traditions really matter.

Tujcalusa

In the west side of Tujcalusa,
country boys still say howdy and ma'am
and they tip their cowboy hats
to salute a lady.

This morning their daily ritual
was interrupted by a subtle nod
from a vaquero with his family.

The Copenhagen smiles disappeared
and memories of the running of the bull
across the deep South decades ago,
brought about a chill at the country store
we call K-Mart.

Alabama sounds Spanish to me
and Tujcalusa reminds me of Yabucoa,
Humacao and other aboriginal names
in Puerto Rico. The familiarity of these names
beckons me.

But this is the Deep South
and no matter how thirsty you are
or how warm it is outside,
it can be a cold place to take a drink of water.

Dalton

Carpet capital of the world, a growing community.
Small enough for the people to still be friendly.

With only one chapter of the council of concerned citizens,
a 21st century evolution of the Knight's of the Ku Klux Klan.

A family oriented town filled with parks;
a lot of the charm left over from the good old days.

Along old Highway 41, a red-stenciled billboard
declares that, *uncontrolled immigration has raised taxes,*
crowded schools, lowered wages and working conditions.
Congress sold us for cheap labor.

A laid back town not too overpopulated,
with the right share of churches for any religion.

A place where the work ethic of America
is being reborn in the hands of southerners
who happen to speak Spanish.

With little snow and 85 degree summers,
close to everything including major cities.

This not so Pleasantville is being transformed
by Latinos who dared to live the dreams advertised
by the same people professing no dogs
and no Mexicans allowed.

Periódicos

Evangelina celebrates her seventy-sixth birthday.
She was born in Colusa County to José and Rocío,
the last child of a five-year marriage.

Generations gather for this special day
to recount their family stories
and to remember every loving soul.

In this household there are photographs
in sepia, in color and in Black & White.

There are clippings in albums
from newspapers that no longer exist.

There is the smell of frijoles and tortas
and there are young men toasting to Mescal.

Joseito is four and tugs at a crochet doily.
A photo album and lamp fall to the floor.
Startled he begins to cry.
Abuelita tells him *is ok mijito tráeme el libro*.
He walks over with the book
and her cashmere hands soothe his tears.

Abuelita Evangelina opens the book
and begins telling Joseito about his name sake.
The voices of the adults in the room fade
as they realize she is talking about her father.

She said my father José was number 575.
He was the last one from 1848 to 1928.

He was lynched and left tied
to a cactus plant
near the train station.

José loved my mother, he loved all of us
and the things they wrote about him
in the newspaper were not true.

She unfolds a newspaper clipping
and reads in a language that no one in that room
under forty had ever heard her speak.

We find that he came to his death
by hanging on the morning of November 10, 1928,
by hands unknown to the jury,
growing out of and the result of the verdict
of the trial in the Superior Court, November 9, 1928,
of which he was charged and found guilty
of the following offenses:

Acting suspiciously, Vagrancy, Being obnoxious,
Throwing stones, Disorderly conduct, Unpopularity,
Trying to vote, Voting for the wrong party,
Demanding respect;

Arguing with a white man, Insulting
a white man, Unruly remarks, Suing
a white man, Testifying against a white man;

Peeping Tom, Enticement, Courting
a white woman, Eloping with white woman,
Living with a white woman, Entering a white
woman's room, Being improper with a white
woman, Adultery, Insulting a white woman,
Frightening a white woman
and Mistaken Identity.
Thus ruining the memory, the chastity
and unimpeachable good character of Mrs. Julia,
a lady of high, pure, and noblest worth.

She holds Joseito's head to her bosom
and rocks him, humming.

The men in the room toast to José.

Home Place

For Dr. Clinton Collins and my classmates of EDU 640

Beyond the shape of my lifespan are mother's
undertones, lingering where we shared birth and death.

There buried in the soil of this small town holler,
I breathe the air of my father.

This enchanting space of my youth belongs
to those who stayed rooted in nature's own language.

I am splintered among memories and emotions
that thread me across generations.

My tragedy is, I have forgotten
how to live, the simple life.

Culture & Politics

Of Jíbaros and Hillbillies

For Minnie Curtis y Castor Rivera

The people of the forest speak with a natural wisdom.
Though thousands of miles apart, they find understanding
in the healing powers of Yerbas Buenas.

Call them Curanderos, Jíbaros and Hillbillies.
Birthed in the land and raised by mountains,
they know what it means to live overshadowed
in a place where so many green things grow.

Scotch-Irish, African-Andalucian and Cherokee-Taíno blood
forged them into poets, composers, and great storytellers.
They delight in the flavor of chocolate gravy,
pimento cheese, and the warmth of fresh cow's milk.

From the method of seasoning a black iron skillet
to the baroque manner in which a man courts a woman,
la pobreza de ser campesino no es lo que nos une
si no, la dignida de una vida sencilla.

Open Mind Tanganyika

For Kianga Ford

Upon your arrival no mystic shepherd
of the Serengeti can dispel the echoes in their eyes
that hazard guesses, *"Ah Black American."*

Nor keep you out of a typecasting audition,
where you perform the title role;
a minority of one, in the land of your DNA.

What a marvelous role you play
to the dozēns of eyes that follow you
across the busy street stage.

From Olduvai Gorge to the streets of Zanzibar;
with the rising sun behind Kilimanjaro
and on location at Mwanza, a city on Lake Victoria.
This community theater plays often
and the casual eye notices the many centuries old
shades of brown in the audience.

Alone, you sail through the wilderness,
to find no rights of passage ceremony
or drums announcing your return,
just the pariah legacy that haunts the old Island.

The Great Rift Valley is more than majestic.
It is the unaccountable time; the sightless forgotten;
the sound of burning flesh; the rattle of wrought iron bells;
the chiming of "half-caste" by school children; the grunt
of old men— abominating your very existence as a sin.

Yet, with an opened mind, you draw guttural strength
from the ancestors who once called this place home.
You know that your bloodline has been chiseled

from under leather, water hoses, and the scars
of an old and unfinished journey.

When at last you depart, from above metal wings
you stare down at this land and dream,
of a transformation for Dar es Salaam.
Praying to mother Africa for a new Tanganyika
one with Dodoma as its redemption.

Generations Deep

For West Virginia Miners

A pain runs through and generations weep
like the very veins of coal they extract.

Folk memories go along with open wounds
only Han can express their guttural twist.

It's hard to learn Jaspers this kind of kinship,
wo-man forged— deep within these mountains.

The silent voices speak through photographs
in the tears of their relative's ghost eyes.

Fingernails burrow deep past the topsoil
to come closer to the land, to their loved ones.

Morena

tún tún tún tún   pop pop
tún tún tún tún   pop pop
tún tún tún tún   pop pop
tún tún tún tún   pop pop

From the rhythm of the drum
was born morena
with the canela, pepper, paprika skin
smelling of oceans west of juracan
wearing the echoes of lonesomeness in her smile.

tún tún tún tún   pop pop
tún tún tún tún   pop pop

From the rhythm of the drum
morena, cultivated gardens of wrinkled fingers,
bent knees and backs, that lifetimes ago stood,
talked, worshiped their creator, the one and only
father, mother, brother, sister cousin of us all.

tún tún tún tún   pop pop
tún tún tún tún   pop pop

From the rhythm of the drum
with the stain of plantains in her veins
morena planted roots in the hearts of stones
at river's bottoms whose winds whispered
Nkosi Sikelel' iAfrika!

morena rhythm

tún tún tún tún   pop pop
tún tún tún tún   pop pop
tún tún tún tún   pop pop
tún tún tún tún   pop pop

Mofongo, Mondongo, Empanadilla,
Morsilla, Ñanicleta, Arepa, Pasteeeeeeeeles!
From a boiling kettle
where fire burns blue, blows red
bits and pieces, ends and ends
all loose in the stew of survival.

morena rhythm

tún tún tún tún   pop pop
tún tún tún tún   pop pop

With the sweetness of coconuts milk in her lips
and memories of footprints washed away by the sea,
morena molded moreno a danza beat of reflejos.

tún tún tún tún   pop pop
tún tún tún tún   pop pop
tún tún tún tún   pop pop
tún tún tún tún   pop pop

From the rhythmmm of the drum—

Morena.

Hatchlings

Pick the flower:
Look for the young and broke in speck towns
where moss grows on the roofs of mud huts,

Establish checkpoints:
Remind him of graveyards filled
with the bodies of his friends.

Prepare the receptacle:
Accuse him of being a spy, of being an infidel.
Shout this over and over and over. Then beat him!
Threatened to kill him in a darken room.
Continue as minutes turn to hours and hours into months.

Pack the fuse:
Once his trembling and crying replaces all manner of language,
let him shake in the darkness; flicker his eyes from four corners,
blame the infidel for the lack of work and poor living conditions.

It's time!

Infuse new words to replace the shouts.
Like the desert lioness— be patient, calm and steady.
Speak of Islam, of paradise, of virgins and duty.

"As a Mute-slim,
you are part of a brotherhood that stretches hundreds of years.
You have an important role to play in the world,
one of prestige and glory."

Offer rewards:
"There are seventy virgins waiting in the Promised Land,
a paradise just for you."

Whisper comfort, promise peace, nourish his temple, and let him rest.
At birth reassure him he is free but some in the brotherhood
are not convinced that he is not a spy; invite him to religious classes;
show him the value of prayer.

Light the fuse:
When he comes to you (and he will) as a Mute-slim
claiming his duty, offer him training,
teach him how to break down an AK47,
about weapons and tactics, and the importance
of keeping his mouth open, when firing a R.P.G.

Make him a chemist, an engineer, and electrician;
indoctrinate him on the how to of artillery shells,
packing plastics and wiring batteries.

Make him a grunt, a Molotov cocktail of death.
Tell him he must prove his resolve.

Blow the fuse:
Reward him with $twenty or $thirty.
Give him a vest, for just in case.
Send him to the market.
Remote detonate.

Up North

The Cessna in my head transformed
into an airliner. Bloomberg TV brought
digital images via the Internet
and we watched them seagull-like
plunge into our homes.

Typical New Yorkers, business as usual,
we tried to focus but our loved ones —
what about our loved ones?

"Get our daughter out of school," I said.
"Why are you still at work? Get out of there! Go!"
"Go to your mothers!" she said, in not so gentle tones.

Wrestling with fear I switched to grunt mode
figuring eight years of Marine Corps'
repetitious training would finally pay off.
Around me, frozen emotions.

"Get out of there!" echoed in my head
and I left, stopping only at the lobby to beg
my co-worker one last time
"Come with me to the Bronx," she stayed.

I marched not thinking about the miles that lie ahead.
Just focusing on the line of us walking north.
Our New York gait was a little different that morning,
the sense of purpose that distinguishes the natives
from the tourist wasn't firm.
The surrealism of the moment
made our movements uncommitted.

We entered central park mathematically calculating
how far the skyscrapers along the edge

would protrude into the park
if they too would have toppled.

Up the path we moved, good Samaritans
we never stop being. On our route,
defeated by the moment on top of rocks people cried,
in disbelief they embraced and the sound we heard
was a whisper in our hearts. We knew.
We felt the same.

And we marched on through Harlem
a world apart. Tired in so many ways.
A gypsy cab running shuttles from the park
to the edge of the water I rode,
until traffic allowed us no further
and I marched again, up north.

Across the bridge into the Bronx,
rode the BX1, passed the old neighborhood.
On the Grand Concourse I struggled to glance
out of the crowded bus and thanked God
Yankee stadium was unharmed.

Soon after I arrived at my mother's apartment,
a place, a neighborhood I knew so well,
yet shaken, I was safe among the family photos
and familiar faces, Up North.

We Who Have Not Fallen

Pain and suffering and I am tired.

Good Morning America reports people have died
in the war.

Bombs, murders, rapes governments stop at nothing.
Muckrakers and Objectivity; another Mayagüez?

The fossils in the news say this will be a quick war;
another Taliban.

Retired generals, who should be playing canasta
talk strategy, attack formations, and tactical advantages.

Get out of my TV Sir!

No one speaks of nationalism when we invade
the self-esteem and Iraqis die.

I know, every mistake, every word—kills too.

AK47s scare up soldiers' lungs and we who have not fallen,
pray for them to breathe—while they fire—while they fight.

Prelude To a Revolution

Red bone, high yella, jet-black, ebony,
copper tone, living learning his-story.
Taking part of Pavlov's classic conditioning.

Show them a pair of Air Force Ones pumps,
designer jackets and Cazzells glasses. Watch them live
in hell, a maze where punishment was/is/will be
random whippings, beatings and killings
for making the wrong/right turn.

Experiment/project what is the difference?
One is in a lab; one is in your neighborhood.
In either case don't forget your tail
or you'll be put in jail where
contaminated subjects end up.

Run, run but you can't hide as long as you got
your brand 566-46-4748 the universal trace.
Colored people have to be odd— they, they have
to be even, straight— a vision to reign supreme.

Break down their spirit the one
Nathan, Nate, Nat Turner used to fight.
So many visions to keep us back,
Methodist, Baptist, Catholic come on!
We're all black.

Run, run back to the motherland and find
the cure for the blind. So that Chaka, Martin
and Rodney can be the last kings to suffer
in this world of sin.

The Panther Within Us

Once upon a time not too long ago
in a ghetto very much like my own.
There lived black men
who rose from the death that was/is oppression;
to live and die for the people;
to bring back power to the people.

There lived men, black
who knew they were brothers
of the Jesús and Wanderer.
Not that savior and that flock
but the makers of that
special kind of living sleep
just for the walking dead.
Men who were weathered by the experience
of asserting their black manhood.
Learning the high price of consciousness
in a world designed for sleepers.

Once upon a time not too long ago
in a ghetto very much like my own.

There lived da' man in the shape of black men
who sold his soul down in Georgia
when johnny lost his fiddle.
Come, check it out! come, check it out!
One bald headed messiah for just
the black race.
Small price to pay by those
who can never be the kind of black men who were
high—on the people
living in shot-gunned houses
so that you and I could break our daily fast.

Once upon a time not too long ago
in a ghetto very much like my own.

There lived women black
who fought for our children and kept us awake
in a world where many of us were/are asleep.
Women very black. Not the color
but the consciousness that feeds the hungry,
heals the wounded, nurtures the soulless,
and shelters the homeless. The kind of black
that cries for freedom and then creates
and orchestrates revolutions,
even when bald-head messiahs
lead us down roads that lead us to— nowhere.

Once upon a time not too long ago
in a ghetto very much like my own.

I heard the shouts:
"I ain't gonna die sliding on no ice."
"I ain't gonna die in no airplane crash."
"I'm gonna die for the people."
"Cause, I live the people."
"Cause, I love the people."

"Power to the people."
"Power to the people."
"Power to the people."

Kill the Landlord

Had a flashback yesterday,
my brotha was gonna
yeah, he was.
Kill the landlord.
That mother...

Who never shows his ass around,
he knows better.
My brotha is watching
and slumlord knows
the what, the why, the when, the how,
he's put a studio size fridge in a five bedroom apt.
Meanwhile, trying to tell us it's standard size.
We may have been fresh off the seven forty seven
but we weren't dumb.

My brotha was gonna
yeah, he was.
Kill the landlord.
That mother...

Had both reps.
Reputation and representative;
neither was worth shit.
Garza was his name and slum dwellings his game.
Ran out the house so fast,
I never seen fat shake like that.

Gonna go tell
¡Me quieren dal! That's right!
No.
That's wrong.
My brotha wasn't gonna— hit you.
My brotha was gonna— yeah he was.
Kill the landlord and his rep.

Couldn't get us a gallon of paint
We needed ten.
We have to order, he said.
But while he spoke there went,
the paint man, I said.
Up the stairs with gallons of paint.

I never seen fat shake like that.
Gonna go tell, we ain't been around
long enough to complain.
My brotha was gonna,
but mamí put on the breaks
she said, we'll buy our own,
we'll paint our own and we did.

No one cares anymore.
They say we're bad blood
circulating conscious thoughts
through those who sleep.
We don't care.
Now that we got our own Frigidaire.

The landlord better not, because
we're gonna, yeah we are.
Kill the landlord.
That mother...

X

For Frank X Walker II

You be my X,
that unknown part of me
that was wandering through the wilderness,
spitting into the wind and taking death defying
leaps, into oceans whose bottoms were stone coffins
for the soon to be departed.

You be my X,
that unknown part of me
left to the free will of her Majesty, creator of us all.
My distant brother torn away
because of your ability to control the storm.

You be my X,
that unknown part of me
that brought order to chaos,
introduced me to Mint Juleps & Bluegrass,
southern cooking, southern ways,
southern gatherings and best of all
southern women.

You be my X,
that unknown part of me
that likes people's company
but not their conversations,
The Cipher that brought
Kwasi & Kwaku full circle.

Homecoming

For Honorée Fanonne Jeffers

In our blood, looping cycles through our veins
a transcendental marker as old as time;
a way of remembering that we are African
making irrelevant misogyny, cultures and nationalities.

Mother Africa's umbilical chord
sings when her children are hurting
and we experience the quickening;
a reconnecting deep within the feeling of angst.

In this hollow so profound our emptiness
cannot be heard but by the rhythm of our heart.
A longing that we cannot explain calls to us,
we know is in our love and in our warmth.

De Pérdida Y Amor

India

I never learned if you were part Taina
or if your parents named you
after the mahogany on your skin.

You hired my blood to subdue me,
to bend my arm across my back
and pucker me up, so that you could
plant a flag on my lips
and declare me your boyfriend.

At your funeral Andrés and Julio
were not your pallbearers, although
they were devoted friends to you and me
when we were ten.

Esta vez, fui yo el que besó esos labios,
fríos como el barro. Quedándome eleto,
buscando en tu rostro aquella memoria,
aquel momento de nuestro encuentro
y al fin arrastré una sonrisa a tu lado.

On my knees I held your mother's hand,
told her how wonderful you were
and how deeply I lamented your departure.

Her trembling hands grasped mine
nodding appreciation and she asked me,
"How did I know you,"
I replied, "*Su hija fue mi primer beso.*"

Oración a Elegüa

Elegüa is the Orisha associated with St. Martin de Porres;
the Orisha of doorways and crossroads

Elegüa
¿A dónde lo llevas?
Tell us about this new world.
¿Qué va ser de su ran kan kan?
Will he play?

Papa Legba
El necesita su música.
We make this offering.
En la montaña escucha nuestra suplicación.
Watch over the fate of us Latinos.

Papa Le Bas
Guardian *de puertos y cruces,*
you called on Tito to return home.
Nuestros ojos con inmenso dolor
understand the nature of our existence.

Exu
¿Cómo arrancamos esta pena de su ausencia?
Solamente queda su memoria.
Tell us what we are to do.
Nosotros sabemos que tú nos diriges.

Eshu
Protege a nuestro Tito.
Celia your brother has arrived.
Tito R esperastes tanto tiempo por tu amigo
Machito! Your students are back!
¿Qué enseñas hoy?
¿Qué enseñas hoy?
¿Qué enseñas hoy?

Inherent

I did not consider the possibility
that I might be attracted to women.

Expected to get married when I reached
the right age was written on my script.

Mother and I were stitching at the foot of her bed
when she unleashed the generational speech
with redness in her eyes.

"You can only be happy if you live a normal life,
one with a husband and children," she said.
Showing me the quilted patch
for the family she had planned for me.

Being attracted to other women was a muted utterance
waived away by a calloused hand
and the power of a culture of subjugation.

"A mother knows these things," she said.

My sorrow fed itself back into me.
A bitter taste, for love was a conditional state
inherent to heterosexism

and I— just wanted a life with those who claimed
that my existence was a blessing; a joy;
an immeasurable gift.

Last Request

She doesn't sense that I am awake
that this pain has knotted my heart and lungs.

It will not be until the alarm echoes
and I failed to react to her third nudge.

The final repulsion will be a gasp
as she slithers from the bed in revulsion.

It will be a while before she can string
together a lifetime of conversations.

I have prayed that this be the way
without embarrassment and in my slumber.

Part of me, will be placed in scented oils
gifted to family, friends and other loved ones.

Some will claim me in sandalwood, others in Maple;
Autumn Harvest will resonate with my southern friends.

What remains, will be sown at the root
of my childhood tamarind tree.

Its supple branches will droop gracefully.
In its fruit I will replicate the red heartwood D.N.A.

At sunrise, during the dry season I will blossom
with a feathery foliage and pink buds.

The fissures in my bark will operate
as water channels for our memories,

and under my canopy we will share the conversations
that survived trapped in our throats.

When I Get Back

It won't be through the canyon of heroes;
there won't be any confetti hovering the skies

or marching bands; crowds will not chant my name
nor will they applaud in adulation;

iconic moments like soldiers kissing women
with curled up legs like guitar strings will be echoes.

A latched door will force me to enter through the
laundry room, where cat litter will trace my footprints.

On a beige sofa I will sit in solitude before retiring
to a corner of the king size bed.

There will be dirty dishes waiting to be clean because
it is my duty, even when I am not around.

Anguish, and depression will strike upon my arrival
yet my four year old will smile and hug me unconditionally.

I will wear the numbness to this existence like a robe
and choose to be a jug-head, best friend with whisky and rum.

What awaits me when I get home
is the life that I am scared to leave.

Election Hoopla

I will not wear campaign buttons.
Or get excited and masturbate
over the outcome of this election.

Neither candidate can fix my marriage or explain
why we don't love each other anymore.

Nor can they dam my mother's tears.
Or assure her that my impending divorce
is not her failure as a mother.

My problems do not fall under an economic theory
that can be stimulated by fifteen hundred dollars.

Will this election forecast the impact
on my son's psyche, when I'm not there
to respond to his mid-summer night's dreams?

If either is elected, how will my teenage daughter change,
After losing her birth father to irresponsibility
and me to irreconcilable differences?

I am going to do carry on with my responsibility
but I cannot get excited about this historic election.
There is too much of the same in its shadows.

A Father's Day Poem

I wish my father had loved me the way I love my son;
unrehearsed, unconditionally and for free.

I wish his heart beat like hummingbirds wings for me.
That I was like the morning dew's touch to him.

That it wasn't the power of prayer that healed my aches
but the strength of his embrace.

That on days like today, I could understand the meaning
of such words as happy and father.

That my love could travel both forward and backwards;
that I had someone to call.

I wish my father had loved me the way I love my son;
around the corners and with a lifetime guarantee.

EZ Stop Diesel Café

Exit 41 on the Bluegrass Parkway, KY

It's late morning the sun has not yet
warmed the tar beneath the tires of the Ford 350.

Inside she sits, window cracked, radio loud enough
to overshadow the song on her lips.

Cigarette smoke curling like brass knuckles
amid the shimmering pink on her left hand.

She drags as if purposely trying to sedate her lungs;
her eyes stare at the princess cut diamond,

a reminder of his promise till death do us part.
Smoke exits her throat, touching her unsettlement.

A glance on the rear view mirror, leads her fingers
to sow through her hair and to words of reassurance.

An instant message speaks softly and she turns off the ignition.
The sound of gravel slowly dispersing makes her smile.

With haste in her hands she grabs her cigarettes and purse.
In his car she feels the gentleness of his touch.

The sound of tires moving on gravel at the Diesel Café
reflect her uneasiness in the rear view mirror.

A Love Poem For West Virginia Gals

For Crystal Good

In Charleston some women are tall,
others come in a rainbow of colors.

They speak sensitively, as if they carried
a yellow Canary in their lungs.

Their love requires no assembly, just
follow the simple directions to their heart.

A pickaxe in the trunk of their car
lets Jaspers know, nothing gets pushover

except the coal on their lips. They take
their bourbon straight and without a blink.

In the office or at sweet water campgrounds;
with pen and paper or a rope in their hand,

they are as comfortable as the stars in the sky.
Don't be confused by the crook in their smile

you might feel the snap of their bite,
if your hand don't come off their hips.

In Charleston some women are tall,
others come in a rainbow of colors.

They speak sensitively, as if they carried
a yellow Canary in their lungs.

Redbone

For Kelly Pendergrast

Night falls:
Consent to tattoos of desire;
to calligraphy sonnets that brogue
of virginal Shakespearean maidens.
Allow for splashes of hieroglyphs,
to flicker seduction in your retinas.
Engrave your self from haunch to toe.
Let the Running of the Bulls brand your
legs with St. Luke's Passion.

Morning comes:
Do not awake with shame in your eyes,
nor pretend that satiety is your companion.
Unleash your apprehension and morality.
Plunge without holy regret
and search the underside of your guilt.

See that we are not being judged,
for this carnal dance.

The Lure

For Rebecca Howell

They met and he was rapt all at once.
Nothing about it was eventful enough
to trigger his lung inflation,

rather the charm in which her cowboy boots
held her calves close, and how one
bended knee rocked over the other.

Enthralled walking away looking over
his shoulder, he asked the mirror
what, was it that brought about this lug?
Poetry was the answer.

Time passed and he danced as she was starring.
He leathered himself hoping she would pull him.

When his chest felt a wind swept moment
he fest like a toreador without red roses
and he wondered if she was his Avispado.

A Ladder

For Charmaine Dixon

I to I we stood,
a shorty you told me I was.

Your orange sliced lips to taste I wanted,
you told me a ladder I would need.

Your custard apple breast to taste I wanted,
you told me a ladder I would need.

To climb your Jamaican tree where the fruit was sweet,
you told me a ladder I would need.

Didn't you know a ladder I would not need,
if eating from the bottom of your tree.

Glossary

Affrilachia – A term coined by Frank X Walker to represent the heritage and claim a space for people of color in the Appalachian Region.

Affrilachian Poets – A group of poets of color who assembled themselves at the University of Kentucky in 1991 and proclaimed the diversity of Appalachia.

Agüela – A rural form of Abuela meaning grandmother.

Anosmia – The inability to perceive odors.

Atronachs – In the gaming world an Atronach is an elemental entity, which derives its powers from the earth, wind, fire, or water.

Avispado – Meaning Cunning. It was the name of the Bull that killed Paquirri one of Spain's greatest bullfighters in 1984.

Batey – was the name given to a special plaza around which the native Caribbean Taino Indians built their settlements. In rural Puerto Rico the front yard is referred to as El Batey.

Bendición – meaning a blessing. Commonly used by Puerto Ricans children before going to bed or by grown ups prior to taking a trip or upon arrival.

Cabrón – A vulgar word implying that a spouse is not being faithful. A most heinous word in Puerto Rican culture.

Caoba – Mahogany wood.

Chomolungma – Means mother goddess of the universe or Mt. Everest.

Curanderos – In Puerto Rico, a curandero (or curandera for a female) is a traditional folk healer or shaman that is dedicated to curing physical and/or spiritual illnesses.

El Don – To have El Don is to have a special gift. An anointment.

Escarmiento – Admonishment.

Estiércol ‑ Manure.

Griot – Is a West African poet, praise singer, and wandering musician, considered a repository of oral tradition.

Guanábana – Soursop, a tropical fruit.

Han – A concept in Korean culture that is sometimes expressed as a lifelong suffering or sorrow. An accute gutteral pain, a state of being, a sadness so deep that tears will not come.

Hillbillie – Is a term referring to people who dwell in rural, mountainous areas of the United States, primarily Appalachia.

Invierno – Meaning winter.

Jasper – Mineral found in the mines of Asheville, North Carolina and the Blue Ridge Mountains. Coveted so much by early miners that the name has been used to refer for those who came to mine it.

Jíbaro – Is a term meaning "hill" or *forest people*, commonly used in Puerto Rico to refer to mountain dwelling peasants, but in modern times as a broader cultural meaning.

Juju – Is a word of West African origin, derived from the French joujou (toy) that refers to the supernatural power ascribed to an object.

Mai – A rural short version of the word mama or mami meaning mother.

Magicka – In the gaming world it is an energy force that allows individuals to cast spells.

Mayagüez – The Mayaguez container ship incident involving the Khmer Rouge government of Cambodia in 1975.

Morena(o) – Colloquial word used by Puerto Ricans to acknowledge and refer to their black heritage. Also, used to refer to people with black or dark hair.

Nkosi Sikelel' iAfrika – "Nkosi Sikelel' iAfrika" ("God Bless Africa" in Xhosa), is part of the joint national anthem of South Africa since 1994, which was originally composed as a hymn by a Methodist mission school in Johannesburg teacher, Enoch Sontonga in 1897.

Ojalá – Spanish for "si Dios quisiera" from the Arabic (law sha'a Allah), Meaning god willing or maybe.

Pangola – Colloquial word used to refer to tall grass areas in Puerto Rico.

Periódicos – Meaning Newspapers.

Piñones – Northeastern section of Puerto Rico. A popular beach destination of the 1970's.

R.P.G. – U.S. military acronym for Rocket Propelled Grenade.

Se quedo eleto – a Puerto Rican euphemism that is short for Esqu(eleto) (skeleton), used to signify one is emotionless like the facial expression of a skeleton.

Taíno – Along with the Carib people they populated the Caribbean Antilles. A branch of the Arawak peoples of Northern Amazonian South America.

Tanganyika – Was an East African territory lying between the Indian Ocean and the largest of the African great lakes: Lake Victoria, Lake Malawi and Lake Tanganyika. It is part of modern day Tanzania.

Tamarindo – Long-lived tropical evergreen tree with a spreading crown and feathery evergreen foliage and fragrant flowers yielding hard yellowish wood and long pods with edible chocolate-colored acidic pulp.

Tuco – Colloquial reference for the remaining part of a limb after amputation.

Tujcalusa – Puerto Rican spelling of phonetic pronunciation for Tuscaloosa, Alabama.

Volky – An affectionate name for the Volkswagen Beatle vehicle of the 1970's in Puerto Rico.

About the Author

Ricardo Nazario y Colón was born in the South Bronx, NYC and raised in Carruzos, Carolina, Puerto Rico.

He is a graduate of DeWitt Clinton High School and has studied at Hudson Valley Community College; Fordham University (Rose Hill); University of Kentucky and Pace University (NYC). He holds a bachelor's degree in Spanish Literature and Latin American Studies, and a Master in Secondary Education. He is a doctoral student in the Education Policy and Evaluation program at the University of Kentucky and lives in Bowling Green, Kentucky where he is the director of the Office of Diversity Programs for Western Kentucky University.

As an undergraduate student he co-founded the Affrilachian Poets — a group of friends who have dedicated the last 20 years of their writing careers, to the aesthetic of making the invisible visible.

Look for Ricardo's poems in the *Louisville Review*, *ArtScene*, *A Hudson View*, *Aphros*, *Southern Poetry Anthology*, *BlazeVox*, *Amphibi.us*, *Eclipsing a Nappy New Millennium Anthology*, *Arts Across Kentucky*, on *Facebook* and on his website at www.lalomadelviento.com.